Anywhere Imaginable




DAVID DEMRO

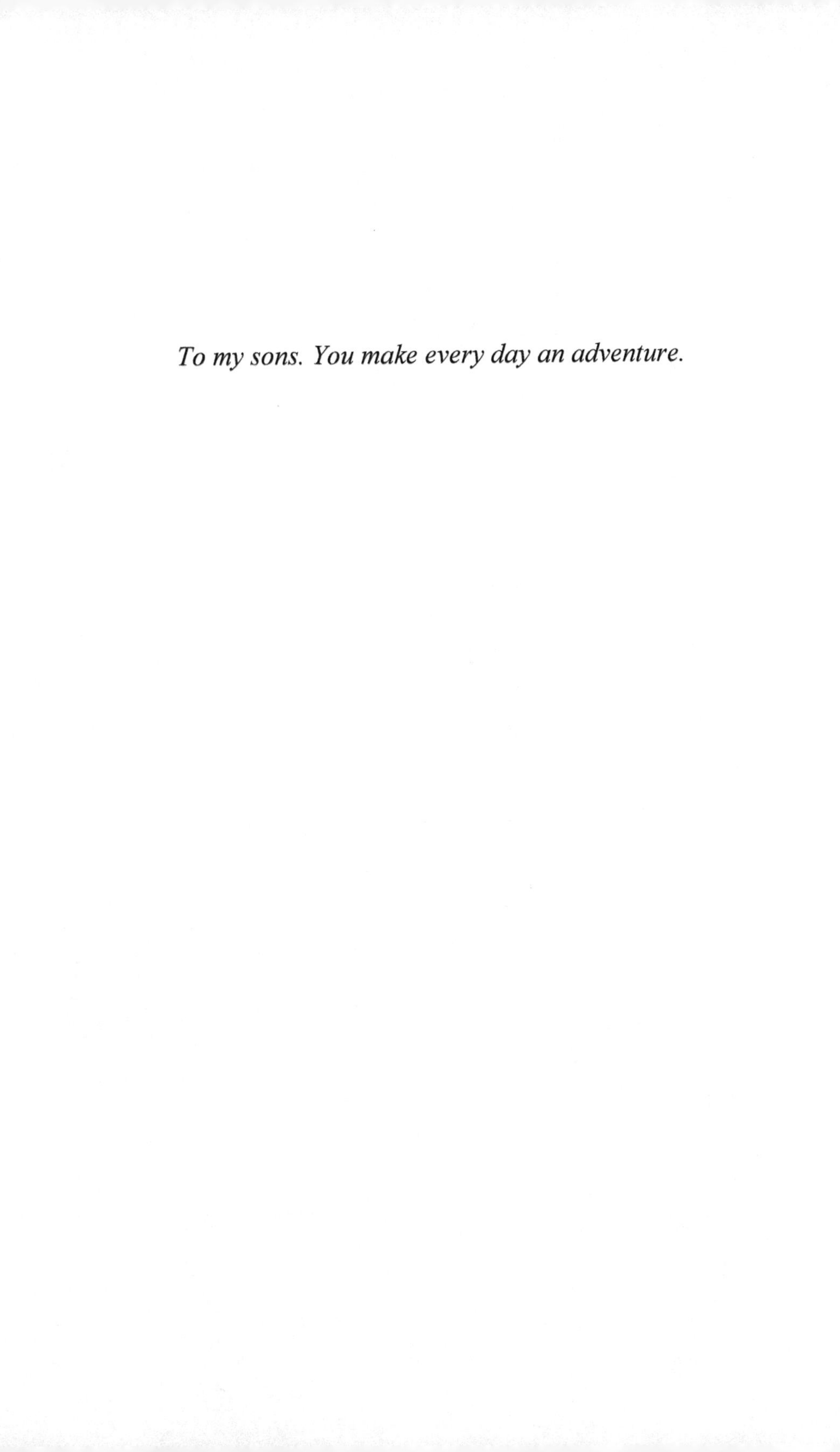

*To my sons. You make every day an adventure.*

# Contents

35.) Dream Rewind

37.) Nightmare

38.) Lost In-Between

39.) The Unwritten

40.) Cooking Rice

41.) Eating Ribs

42.) WeFinallyMadeIt

44.) Don't Go to the Casino Hold'em Table on a Weekday

46.) Dear Apt. G

48.) The Reacher

49.) I Stand

50.) Pearl

52.) She Smiled and Said

53.) Very Pleasant

54.) Bulletproof

56.) Dreaming of Immortality

57.) Yard Sale

58.) Leukemia

59.) Christmas In August

60.) Viking Funeral

61.) He Stood There When the Earth Was Whole

62.) Burned

63.) I'll Hold Your Hand

64.) Tomb Sweeper

65.) Visitation

66.) Rejection Letters

67.) From My Breakfast Barstool

68.) Y'all

69.) Geography

70.) Arrivals

71.) Departures

72.) Terminal Parking

74.) Lost In Thought

75.) Are You This Many

76.) Eating Ice Cream in the Flames

77.) Zombie

78.) How to Stop a Bad Guy (by a Three-Year-Old)

79.) To The Moon

81.) The Ascent of Art Hill

82.) When a Family of Five Doesn't Eat Before a Lookouts Game

83.) 100 Days of School

84.) 100 Smiley Faces

85.) Where Was the Level

87.) Memory

88.) Yesterday

89.) Shadow Puppets

90.) The Sprinkle King

91.) 1 am

92.) Taxidermy

93.) Anywhere Imaginable

94.) Pumpkin Chunkin'

96.) In a Sea of Mustard

98.) Someone Drugged My Tacos

99.) Chicken Nuggets

100.) The Hungry Masseuse

101.) There Was Comfort in Our Couch

102.) Remain Calm

103.) Balconies

105.) Concrete Jungle

106.) Raccoon Mountain

107.) The Dandelion Hunter

108.) Without a Poem on the Page

109.) Corona Flattop

*Ah! The Bookstore…*

It's been so long
that I forgot
how elating

the aromatic smell of
new books
can be,

and as I wander
near the espresso bar
I realize

I still can't decide
which I prefer more:
the smell of new books

or fresh-brewed espresso,
but there's no need
to decide now

because I'm
basking in both at
the bookstore.

*Fonts*


I'll never be able to take
a Comic Sans resume seriously

and can still picture my dad's handwriting
on the backs of unopened envelopes in

**FELT TIP PERMANENT MARKER
ALL CAPS - BOLD**

and still can't decide which I prefer more for this poem:
Cambria or Times New Roman

*but either way, I appreciate
the various use of italics (available with most fonts)*

and then there's my favorite font on those days
I don't feel like reading much at all: illegible.

*Staccato*


When you said you found the remains of
a burned piano in your yard
I imagined holding a white piano key,

charred at the edges,

and was transported to the years of my
early childhood piano lessons,
the countless hours of trying to

perfect a simple song,

and my teacher explaining
the purpose of the dot
over a musical note:

*Press it quick as if the key is burning hot.*

I was sitting on a piano bench,
pulled up to a piano that was engulfed in flames,
playing every note in

staccato.

*No Poets*

Scrolling through
home and
rental listings
on Zillow:

no pets,
no kids,
no evictions,
no felons,
no bankruptcies,
no poets.

There's just
no winning
these days
(no… wait,
no poets?):

No exceptions!

*The Allure*

Finally made it to the coffee shop
to get some writing in,
and now that I'm here,

I'm wondering if it was just
the allure of writing here
instead of the act of writing itself.

I wonder if the same can be said
of that inviting bench
on the pedestrian bridge

in Chattanooga
overlooking the Tennessee River,
but here I am

filling these lines with words
so maybe there's more to
the allure after all.

I'll consider the Iced Doppio
with Sweet Cream Cold Foam
an added bonus.

*From the Balcony at Twin Lakes*


Fish submerged like
submarines in clear water,

the startling
buzz

as a Ruby-throated
Hummingbird flies by,

squirrels as loud as bears
rustle leaves

across the lake,
a cool spring breeze

brings
goosebumps

as the refreshing
sights and sounds

of nature
bring relief.

*Birders*


A couple emerged from the woods
as my wife and I
ate fast food from a paper bag
at a picnic table
next to the Kankakee River.

"Are you Birders too?" they asked.

(In hindsight, it must've been
the lack of fishing poles.)
I took a big bite of food,
hoping my wife would answer,
as I had no clue what a Birder was.

They had binoculars
dangling from their necks,
notebooks in-hand,
and were reading a description of a bird call
they thought they heard nearby.

I wondered what the description
of a bird call looked like in print.
5 years later and 585 miles away,
I anticipate my wife and I
will soon find out.

We happen to be moving near
a Bird Sanctuary

on Signal Mountain,
and I can't think of a better time
to walk around town with binoculars

dangling from our necks,
notebooks in-hand,
trying to match the sound of a bird call
to its mysteriously printed counterpart
while asking the neighbors,

"Are you Birders too?"

*Card Catalog*


The librarian was always there,
watching over her glasses,
silently signaling to my brother and me
to quiet down when we were making too much noise
which was every time we entered the library.

And then one day,
I did not return
for many years.

When I finally did return
to the familiar place,
while on assignment,
I walked to the card catalog
which remained unmoved
and pulled open an empty drawer.

This caught me by surprise, and
I opened another empty drawer
followed by another
and another,
filling the silent library with noise
that felt as loud as my brother and I had made
when we were children.

I looked up in confusion
and met eyes with the librarian
who was watching over her glasses.

She silently signaled towards the computers
that now serve as the card catalog.

*SSDD*


I had to Google this acronym,
and now I feel old
AF.

*The Headline Read...*


"To Save Money,
Maybe You Should Skip Breakfast"

*What a great idea!*
I thought to myself.

While we're at it,
why not just skip
lunch and dinner too?

And I imagine
dessert
is already off the table.

I can't think of a better way
for society to "thrive" than
choosing starvation
in order to keep up with inflation

all while continuing to pay
the bills.

*Profits Over People*


"Another quarter in the red," they said,
the company surgeon deciding
where and who to cut,

when all I really want to do
is be guided carelessly and curiously
down the road,

hand-in-hand with my
two-year old leading the way.
He tugs my pant leg to stop us,

and I look down
to see him pointing up
saying, "Look, the moon! The moon!"

We stand still, as if frozen in time
among a hurried crowd of suits,
observing the moon.

Meanwhile, corporations stay busy
vying for "Best of…" awards,
positioning themselves to be

a picture-perfect employer;
yet in the dark they cut,
cut,

cut.

*Fired*


I was fired last week.
*Not to worry*
I thought to myself,
I'll just float some applications out there.

Number of applicants for this opening:
7,450
3,750
75 (posted 20 minutes ago)

Well… that's not good.
Let's see how unemployment works.

Maximum allowance:
$275 per week (if approved)

Well… that's not good either.

*Warm Clothes*


*I am present,*
trying my best to find comfort
in the warmth of clothes
being pulled from the dryer
at the buzzer,

and not dwelling too long
on more pressing matters
like, *Will I get a response*
*to one of my daily*
*job applications?* or,

*Where will my family and I go*
*if we can't make rent*
*this month...*
*next week...*
*tomorrow?*

## Boardroom Etiquette

The smell and smoothness of
this new black leather Traveler's Notebook
reminds me of my childhood
Rawlings baseball glove.

The glove would be out of place
in the boardroom
much like the dollar store notebook
that I brought to the last meeting.

My boss caught a glance of the generic
composition notebook as I flipped it open, and
his fraction-of-a-second facial expression said,
*Now you know.*

And in case you don't know,
dear reader, everyone brings a
black leather folio to the boardroom with
business cards tucked into a pocket on the inside cover
(I've yet to receive my business cards).

While I won't be joining my clients
in writing on full-sized legal pads,
this notebook will blend well enough,
travel even better, and serve as a great conversation starter,

for those in the know.

*A Coffee Pot at Your Cubicle*


A coffee pot at your cubicle
is the true testament of dedication
to the workplace,
and while I appreciated your offer
of any pick from various flavors
I much prefer my walk
to the sometimes decent
and mostly awful
medium roast breakroom coffee
where I catch a glimpse outside
through a partially shaded window
and wonder what I'd be doing
if I wasn't here today,
or any working day,
before returning to my desk.

*The Magician's Coat*


I don't know what possessed me
to buy this ridiculous black pea coat
with the over-exaggerated pointed collar.

When I appear at work
my colleagues stare as if I'm about to
pull a rabbit out from beneath

my nonexistent top hat
or reveal the Ace up my sleeve,
but tomorrow I'll surprise them

by not appearing at all.
They'll point at my empty desk and say,

*A true Houdini that one is*
*with his ridiculous magician's coat.*

*4 am*


I awake to a
truck beeping at
the crack of dawn

wondering,
like I always do
when I awake to

a beeping truck,
whether I've taken out
the trash

and realize
I can rest easy
because it's Tuesday

and not Friday,
but
Friday would be nice,

and what was that truck
if not a garbage truck,
and will I ever

get back
to sleep
tonight?

*The Forgotten*


I wrote a poem
in my mind last night and
fell asleep before writing it down.

This is not that poem.

*Aftermath, Tornado*


drops of rain on photos
scattered outside on the ground,
tears in everyone's eyes

*Photo Finish*


We never met,
Bukowski and I,
but I imagine us
sitting at the racetrack
catching up on everything
and nothing at all,

exchanging the occasional poem
scrawled out on paper
to silently read
over the sound of
horse hooves
beating the earth,

and taking in the moment
when words
have me on the edge
of my seat

like a photo finish

that fleeting feeling
gone
in a flash.

*Nomophobia*



Heads down
all day and night
staring at screens aglow.

Backs bowed in
obedience and fear.
When life's light

leaves our eyes,
we look up
with wonder.

*Autocorrect*

You're*

> Two latte
> all ready judging
> your gram more

*Scrolling*

Scrolling
through social media
looking for…

what?

A flash of
brilliance?

A shimmer of
delight?

Both of which can be found
within the walls of my own home
if I just set down my phone.

Walking along the travelator
between walls of 3x3
pastel-colored squares,
each bordered in white,

like an atom
traveling between the pages of
the Color Index book
exploring the color palette of life.

*A Vicious Cycle*



Concrete and people;
cracks and imperfections.

My lack of recollections?
Boredom; no delight.

Tired of the fight:
sifting for passions;

winding up with
throwing stones.

Left alone -
skipping along until I've

drowned.
Resting on the riverbed;

longing to be dredged.
Observing

still and silent.
Throw me once more into the light.

*The Fastest Buckets… Ever.*


Baristas calling out names
faster than Mr. Riner
taking 4th grade attendance,

thirsty outstretched arms
grasping at cups of happiness -
taken one sip at a time,

and I'm wondering,
*Are half these names made up*
*to get more people in line*

*by having them take note*
*of the quick turnaround time?*
Mike, Medicine Ball.

Karen, Flat White.
David (my drink name
must be too long to call out;

Iced Doppio with Sweet Cream Cold Foam
in case you happen to be in line
and know where to find me).

Mike,
Mike,
Mike…

## The State of Drive Thru Customization

Can I get a double cheeseburger
with finely diced onions,
shredded pickles,
cheese halved and quartered,
ketchup in the shape of a smiley face
and mustard in the shape of the sun
with some extra yellow rays all around
for good measure?

*Some Things Never Change*


Anything change since I've been gone? Jimmy asked,
as he hopped in my five speed Mustang
outside Midway Airport.

Yeah, I learned how to drive stick, I said,
before letting the clutch out too fast
and killing the engine.

*Visiting My Hometown*


Coming in for a landing
like the nose of a lead pencil
approaching the Start line of a maze,

lead line gliding
down the runway,
and before I know it

I'm off to the races
in a rental car
making my way down memory lane:

the old 7-Eleven (all boarded up now)
the secret fishing spot at the unnamed reservoir
the all-you-can eat breakfast joint nearby

the (now overgrown) ballfields where we spent our childhood
the old schools which don't seem all that much different
from the outside

my old house
the houses of family and friends
the houses my dad built

brick by old brick
and before I know it
it's time to turn back

and make my way to the Finish,
and I wonder if I'll ever find myself
above the clouds again

one
last
time.

*Random Thoughts of Nostalgia*


I'm feeling nostalgic
and spinning this mouse wheel
brings me back

to rolling the throttle on the good ol' CB750
(and let's not forget the short-lived CX500 café project bike)
and my dad's old record player setup,

all the backlit knobs, wheels, and sliders
had the makings of a spaceship console,
and as I contemplate scooping up a record player of my own

for old times' sake
I suddenly flash back to my brother and me
using my dad's old records as Frisbees

(I sure hope he's not reading this now)
and I wonder how this MCM roll top desk
will look in my bedroom?

Regardless, every writer needs an unplugged workspace
free from the tangles of the world wide web,
a place where I'm too easily lost

in everyone else's experiences
(and in online shopping),
instead of being out and about in the world

living it up -
just like we did
in the good ol' days.

*Dream Rewind*


I've been eaten by wild animals.
I've fallen from mountains.
I've been hit by

trains
planes
automobiles.

I've been shot at
point blank
and bombed

for good measure.
Sometimes I don't
awake

and watch as my spirit
rises up and leaves.
Other times,

I am the spirit
traveling through time and
space.

Once, I was
reborn.
The details…

not quite clear;
then fast forward through
birth to

(then)
present day
wondering if I was actually awake

or if it was still part of the dream –
a dream within a dream?
I can control them now,

the dreams,
Dream Rewind,
but it only works

when I realize I'm dreaming.
Sometimes I wonder if
I'll get stuck

rewinding and living out
different outcomes for all eternity.
Maybe I'll see you there.

*Nightmare*


scared to bleed too loud
red dripping splatters night's leaves
they turn and face me

*Lost In-between*


I often feel lost
floating through life

trapped
somewhere between

chasing money and
chasing dreams.

## The Unwritten

I've penned many
pages in my mind
(perhaps a full collection?),
unspoken
hard truths
that sometimes have me
wondering
if I'm living
a lie.

If there's anyone
I should be
completely
open and honest with,
it's you
my dear reader,
but I've said too much
already.

*Cooking Rice*


I thought it was steam
evacuating from the pot of rice,
but the smoke-filled house
suggests otherwise.

*Eating Ribs*


I'd answer your text
if it wasn't for my
saucy fingers.

*WeFinallyMadeIt*

My brother and I watched
the row of white squares
slowly turn blue
one after another
as obnoxious fax-like noises
garbled through PC speakers.

Once online,
we spent hours downloading a game
and again looked on
as the squares slowly changed colors
nearing the end of the download bar.

Once the download was complete
we attempted to play
player vs player
on dialup.

We lagged the whole game through,
every game,
thinking it was normal:

interrupted gameplay
consumed by
the circle of death.

Our adversaries would sometimes quit

giving us a free win
for our highspeed ignorance.

This was it.
We were in.

Username:
WeFinallyMadeIt

except for Friday evenings
which is the start of the weekend
in casino days.

Don't mix chips
with the fish at the table
even if you hit the better flop

bad beats
beginners luck
you get the drop

and don't splash the pot
I repeat, don't splash the pot
or you risk getting kicked from the table.

Find the drunks
sinking drinks
and their bank accounts

between every few hands
seemingly without a care in the world -
that's where the easy money is,

and you'll know I've finally made it
in some way, shape, or form
when I'm the drunk

and you're the one
raking in
the chips.

*Dear Apt. G*


We walked past the apartment mailboxes,
A through L,
all adjoined and each with their own lock,
made our way up to Apt. H,
and found an envelope taped to the door
with a note on it that read:

*I'm not sure if this belongs to you*
*but it was in my mailbox. (Apt. G)*

I looked at who the envelope was addressed to
expecting to see Apt. H,
but it was addressed to Apt. G.
I began to wonder why Apt. G thought this mail might be ours,
and in my mind I wrote back:

*Dear Apt. G,*

*I'm assuming you thought this was ours*
*instead of A, B, C, D, E, F, I, J, K, or L's*
*because H comes after G.*

*I'm also assuming this mail addressed to Apt. G*
*that was placed with the rest of the Apt. G mail*
*in the Apt. G mailbox*
*belongs to someone who used to live in Apt G.*

*When we get this type of mail*
*we cross out the address,*
*write return to sender on the envelope,*
*and drop it in the outgoing mail. (Apt. H)*

*The Reacher*

I am the reacher,
a Monarch emerging from its outgrown chrysalis
anxiously fluttering,
gently falling through a sunlit sky.

Wings spread to dry, wishing my orange and black and spotted
white/
did not contrast
so scabrously against spring's green grass,
attracting birds of prey.

For they know all too well the ephemeral moment
in which the reacher lie.
The Monarch hopes ephemeral metamorphosize
forming two eternal souls:

two reachers you and I.

Lost are the confines of my fail-safe chrysalis,
and with the kiss of a hand and a breath of air against my wings
a Monarch takes flight.
I am the reacher;

to you I fly.

*I Stand*


I stand where the odor of fish meets the aroma of coffee,
where occasional beams of the sun ignite $5 bouquets,
where the pitter-patter of raindrops disappear into the bay.

I stand where patchy fog gives way to Mt. Rainier,
where the tip of the Space Needle aerates an overcast sky,
where drops of rain return mid-day from Puget Sound.

I stand with you -
where happiness is never lost and always found.

*Pearl*

Cannons of thunder
rumble night skies.
Streaks of white lightning
expose high flying tides.
Waves of Blue Moon
pour down in me car.
"Accelerate to 32 knots;
we must get to the bar!"

"A vortex, Captain,
starboard side!"
"Fetch me the spyglass.
I can't see with me eye."
I peer through the lenses
to bring the sea monster closer,
and me eye tenses.
"I mustn't be sober."

My heart drops like the ship's log
pulled down by the vortical swirl.
Within the turbulent flow shines my love
in the form of a pearl.
I cast out me net
to pull you aboard,
but you slip through the mesh.
"Man overboard!"

I swim towards the axis
with all me might.
"I'm not… much of a… swimmer,
but I got lots of fight!"
I reach out and grab you;
clench my fist round you tightly.
Your lustrous hues
shine evermore brightly.

The vortex recesses
back into the sea.
Your pearl iridescence
takes on a human body.
No more high-flying tides,
no lightning; no thunder.
Just you and me love.
Me most treasurous plunder.

## She Smiled and Said

She smiled and said,
*Write me a poem.*
My fingers fumbled between keys
searching for words that ceased to exist.

*Very Pleasant*


I pulled up my virtual chart
after a doctor's visit
and bragged to my wife
about how they described me as
very pleasant.

She laughed and said
*My post-visit notes*
*say the same thing about me.*

It was then
that we realized
the notes
were all
a lie.

*Bulletproof*

It was well past dark,
bugs had been
swarming
the streetlights
for hours,
and I bargained
with my old man
to let me
ride
my new bike
one more time,
just one more time
around
the block.

I heard
fireworks
as I rode
but did not see them.

I raced up
the drive
to inform my dad
thinking we'd
pull out the lawn chairs,
enjoy the show.

He quickly
led me to the
front
of his old yellow pickup
"… to hide
behind the engine bay
where the bullets
can't pass through."

I still wanted to watch.

*Dreaming of Immortality*


Is this how Achilles felt?
Alone,
wielding his sword,
spilling red blood
on the battlefield?

I think to myself
while dreaming of immortality,
wielding my pen,
spilling black ink
on the page.

*Yard Sale*

I watched a
gray haired man
walk from his old
white Mercury,

trunk left open,

carrying a yard sale sign,
red and white,
attached
to a wooden stake.

I realized he was preparing
to bury
his final stake
into the earth

and began to wonder

how I'd feel
in that moment,
what possessions
I'd have left

scattered about
the yard.

*Leukemia*


I hardly recognized you
when I walked into your room.

Wires and tubes led
from all around and
disappeared beneath your sheets.

Your bare arms of skin and bone
lay still on your decaying frame.

I felt as if there was an
invisible wall between us,
a wall separating life
and death, but
I didn't come here to be removed.

I'm here to be a refreshing face
from the days of old
before you were diagnosed
with cancer.

*Christmas In August*


The summer yule log burned
on the tv mounted above the fireplace
as Christmas music played,
and his shaky outstretched arm
grasped gifts neatly wrapped in paper and bows.

I considered it more of a farewell party,
but that may have been too morbid for some,
and definitely more depressing for everyone, than
Christmas in August,
but we all knew what this really was:

death surrounded by crumpled piles of wrapping paper.
I imagined him neatly wrapped in a fresh pressed suit,
resting on the soft interior lining of a coffin,
ready to be delivered.
The tag read,

*From: Us*
*To: God*

*Viking Funeral*

Gusts of fall
send a withered leaf
sailing through pumpkin-scented skies.

Death
rides the river's current;
orange and yellow kin dance

in the trees above.
Their reflections set fire to the vessel
disappearing around the bend.

## *He Stood There When the Earth Was Whole*

He stood there when the earth was whole,
before the rim of the hollowed sandbox was charred;
before you pushed the button from afar.
I don't understand why you did it.

Why did you do it?
Send the earth up like egg yolk,
bursting out of its shell,
lighting up the dark desert sky.

On the surface he was still intact.
Insides? Scrambled.
He was driving the Humvee
before you flipped it on its side;

before you made the air exhale out torn tires
and his last breath leak slowly from his lungs.

*Burned*


I sure miss that old breakfast bar
and the occasional run-ins with Uncle Mike
(who preferred a solo seat
at an otherwise empty table).

They've both been burned to ashes.

*I'll Hold Your Hand*


*I'll hold your hand before you die;*
*I'll hold your hand to God with you.*

And I thought of all the stiff hands
I've held over the years,
the young and old alike,
some long-lived and wrinkled,
some too soft and smooth,
and others that I never did see through
those mysterious pearly gates.

*Tomb Sweeper*


may this dust on stone
my broom sweep until we meet
on the other side

*Visitation*

Most of my friends have
kicked the bucket
by now,
and a few remain
that I see every
year or three.

Outside of that,
I mostly hang out with my
favorite poets
(through their books and not
in the flesh, of course).

Most recently,
I've been enjoying
late night drinks
with Bukowski,

and Billy Collins
likes to visit
most afternoons –
particularly on those perfect
early spring days,

and as I sit here writing between naps,
I wonder who might visit today?

Rejected
Rejected
Rejected
Rejected
Rejected
Rejected
Rejected
Rejected
Rejected
Rejected
Rejected
Rejected
Rejected
Rejected
Rejected
Rejected
Rejected
Rejected
Rejected
Rejected
Rejected
Rejected
Rejected
Rejected
Rejected
Rejected
Rejected
Accepted

*From My Breakfast Barstool*

From my breakfast barstool
I see the other side of the restaurant.
The real side can't be seen from a table or a booth
where groups of family and friends only notice the white
waitresses' fronts./

They don't see the black tattooed cook
peering through the round glass kitchen door window.
They don't see the Mexican bus woman's terrified look
when the Greek owner picks up a creamer bowl.

They don't see the amusing faces the cook, bus, and waitresses
make/
when they break rules the owner forgets
serving me a side of full-sized pancakes.
Maybe he "forgets" in hopes that I keep their secrets.

So when the owner asks, "How is everything?"
I smile and say, "Amazing."

*Y'all...*


has come to be my favorite greeting;
yes, even after giving Wags a hard time
when he brought his Texas drawl

up north,
but after going on 5 years
in Tennessee myself

y'all
just seems to make
the most sense.

Especially given the current state
of pronouns like
he, she, they…

which, if used improperly,
can cause some problems,
but not with y'all!

*Geography*


I became a national traveler in first grade,
the grade students graduated to the big playground
on the other side of the school where

a long yellow line divided the blacktop,
(though I don't recall why),
and the yellow outlines of states

formed a map of the United States.
I'd hop from state to state,
traveling through them all in one recess,

except for the one state that was rumored to be missing.
Maybe it was East Dakota or West Carolina,
or was it closer to the northeastern part of the map

(a place I still don't frequent as often)
near North Virginia?
It was hard to determine as a geographically challenged first
grader/

and even more difficult to recall now
as I study a map
trying to remember.

*Arrivals*


For my birthday,
let's plan nothing at all.

There are already so many plans in life
that making one more feels exhausting.

Let's just head out to anywhere
and figure out what's next when we arrive.

There are days
where life
has beat the living

right out of me
my mind
drifting away

on autopilot
trying to find its way
back home

in an attempt
to not be too quick
in joining the departed.

*Terminal Parking*


Not the sign
I want to be greeted by
when parking at the airport,

and why do they call it
terminal anyways?
But if this is my final parking place

then I suppose I can worry less
about whether I should take my parking ticket
or leave it on the dash,

and I'm not at all concerned
about where I'll store my personal bag
with there being no plane seat in front of me,

7B,
the only seat not behind another
except for those

at the very front of first class,
and speaking of first class,
I'm right behind them,

drawn curtain in my face.
I guess it's there
to shade my eyes

from the backs of
first class passengers' heads
as if my leer alone

might downgrade them
to boarding group 3,
but there's no need

to think much more on that now
because I'm parked in
terminal parking.

*Lost In Thought*


My kids yell at me
to turn off the GPS
when they know where we're at,
but my mind tends to wander
while I drive.

One minute I'm a block away.
The next? Two or three cities
or states down the road
with no recollection of how I got there.

Wait… where are we?
I forgot where I was going with this.

## Are You This Many

*Are you this many, Daddy?*
my four-year-old son asks
holding up all his fingers
on both hands.

*Nope.*
*I'm more than that.*

*How about his many?*
he asks
holding up both
hands and feet
while sitting on the ground,
a smile on his face.

*More than that.*

*All of the peoples'*
*fingers and toes*
*in the whole wide world?*
he asks with concern.

*Well...*
*not quite that old.*

*Eating Ice Cream in the Flames*


"Did you have fun with me today, Daddy?"
My three-year-old son seems so sweet and selfless…
until he threatens to burn down Oberweis

because he wants to go to Cold Stone.
I wonder if he'll use a more peaceful means of problem solving
or grow up to be a pyro?

I'll love him either way,
even if we spend our future days
eating ice cream in the flames.

*Zombie*


*Can we play zombie, Dad?*
my five-year-old son asks
as we pull up to the park.
I open the child-lock door
and yell, *AAAARRRRRGH*...

Both of my kids
shoot out the car,
sprint down a sidewalk
that runs parallel
to a tall stone wall,

and disappear
around a turn
through the arched entryway
of the park
while laughing and screaming,

*Zombie! Zombie!*
I limp down the sidewalk in pursuit,
turn through the entryway,
and am greeted with
partially curious, partially terrified

parental gazes.
They return to their phones
as I yell, *AAAARRRRRGH*...
while chasing my barefoot kids
up the slide.

*How to Stop a Bad Guy (by a Three-Year-Old)*


Dad, if the bad guys get back up
you'll have to take their bones out.

*To The Moon*


The acorns must've all fallen by now.
I no longer hear them
bouncing like marbles
atop the roof
then rolling
rolling
down
like the sound of a pinball
falling into its launcher.

I head out near the
end of the day and
catch a glimpse of the
creamsicle colored sun
between slivers of distant
silhouetted trees
while one kid jumps in piles of leaves,
another sits in them contently, and
another tilts his head back
while swinging on the swing.

I see him observe the bare branches overhead,
and he's no longer yelling,
*Push me high so I can reach the leaves!*

He doesn't have his imaginary space helmet on
so I pass him the one I keep in my pocket
for times like these,

when it's time to get launched
to outer space.

*It's rainbow colored,* he says
as he places it on his head.

Then he closes his eyes tight,
as if preparing for takeoff, and
I wonder what he envisions
as he's laughing
to the moon.

*The Ascent of Art Hill*

I look up,
after a few steps into the ascent of Art Hill,
searching for a launch point,

and begin pulling my kids on a sled
to where the Apotheosis of St. Louis stands tall above the snow.
I wonder if the statue will ever break loose from its base

and watch as he suddenly slides past us on his bronze horse;
they leap over precautionary hay bales at the bottom of the hill
and disappear into the Grand Basin.

*When a Family of Five Doesn't Eat Before a Lookouts
Baseball Game*


1 hotdog
2 brats
2 cotton candies
1 frozen lemonade
1 frozen blue drink
a popcorn
3 bottles of water

1 hotdog
a beer

2 funnel cakes
a chili & cheese nacho
with a side of jalapenos

a popcorn
2 slices of pizza

2 Cookies 'N Cream Dippin' Dots

and a good time

Hey Dad, what's that building
over there?

That one? That's a college Son.

I don't want to go to college Dad.

Don't you think you're a little young
for us to be having this conversation?

But Dad, I already completed
100 days of school.
100 days!

Well kid…
you only have about
another 20 years to go…

…

*100 Smiley Faces*


My son receives a smiley face,
a straight face,
or a sad face
each day
depending on his school behavior,
and we agreed that he'd
earn a prize
at 20 smiley faces.

Today, he left with
17 smiley faces.

When he returned
from school he said,
*Dad! I got 100 smiley faces!*

*No way! Let me see!*
He pulled out an assignment
and at the top was written
100 followed by a smiley face,
100 smiley faces.

*Where Was the Level*


I couldn't find the level
when I needed to
evenly hang curtain rods,

and it evaded me again
when hanging pictures
of our kids,

my wife in the far end of the room
directing me:
*a little to the right,*

*a little to the left,*
but today,
my five-year-old son

seemed to have willed the level
out of thin air
right before my eyes.

"Where did you find that?"
"It was in my pocket."
"No, really. I looked everywhere.

"Where did you find it?"
"It was in my pocket,"
as if I wouldn't have noticed

the four-foot
neon green level
emerging from his pocket.

I immediately took to
checking the recently
hung pictures

which didn't seem quite right
to the naked eye
and were off by

a good half-inch.
Next on the list is a
properly sized storage organizer.

Now, if I can
just find the
tape measure.

*Memory*


The excitement of a three-year-old
flipping over playing cards
and seeing they have matched a pair
sure is something worth remembering.

*Yesterday*


I often half-joke
that life feels like
one long year,

but my 4-year-old son
has taken time perception
to a new level

with life being
one long day
by referring to

any day
before today as
yesterday.

*Shadow Puppets*


Four has been a violent age for my son
who enjoyed beating me up all day

and then destroying my shadow puppets
that emerged on the wall

when writing this poem by flashlight
in the night.

*The Sprinkle King*


The best way to ensure my kids
aren't tearing up other areas of the house
while my wife and I clean

is to get them involved.
Their favorite cleaning activity is sprinkling carpet cleaner,
and they argue over who gets to be

The Sprinkle King
by shouting *I want to be The Sprinkle King!*
*No, I want to be The Sprinkle King!*

The box of carpet cleaner
is bestowed upon the winner,
and The Sprinkle King victoriously sprinkles

small piles of scented powder through our home.
When I notice large areas absent of carpet cleaner
I shout *I want to be The Sprinkle King!*

in hopes that they'll forfeit their rights
so I can quickly finish the job
and move on with our day.

*1 am*

It's 1 am
on a Sunday night, and
I'm sipping coffee
wondering
how much I'll miss these days
and whether something else
(besides kids)
will have me writing
so late
into the night.

*Taxidermy*


My two-year-old pressed his nose against a glass partition
and began naming dead animals,
meticulously mounted,

eerily displayed on the other side.
Squirrel, duck, and other small game
aimlessly stared with unflinching glass eyes.

I doubt this is what he envisioned for me,
at age three, when he said,
*I'm going to keep you forever,*

but I imagined myself armatured,
staring down the barrel of a pen in one hand,
holding a notebook in the other,

writing this poem,
as he points through the glass at me and says,
*That's my Dad!*

*Anywhere Imaginable*

Watching my three-year-old son
spinning in circles
trying to slip his arm through
the second strap of my backpack,
like a puppy chasing its tail,
because it's time to go to
nowhere in particular and
anywhere imaginable.

*Pumpkin Chunkin'*


"Fire!"

A trebuchet lets out a
*clachunk*
as a pumpkin is launched
downrange
over several pink yard flags
spread in 10-yard increments.

The pumpkin bursts
onto the earth and
lets out a booming bellow
that echoes through my chest.

Pumpkin chunkin'
just might be my
favorite cub scout activity,
I think to myself,
(well... aside from the
pinewood derby, of course).

I can't believe I never knew
such a thing existed,
and how do you say
trebuchet?

"Fire!"

A *clachunk*
brings me back to reality
as I watch another pumpkin
sail
across the sky.

*In a Sea of Mustard*


Boat season has ended
which means the brave and/or
ignorant souls are
embarking on their biannual
towing of the boats.

I observe them,
one-by-one,
driving
all up in the mustard,
as I like to call it.

At least they have an excuse,
I suppose,
as opposed to those
with just themselves
and a tightly gripped phone in tow.

I'm on extra high alert
when riding my K75
up and down the mountain,
attempting to avoid decapitation
around blind corners.

Sure enough,
here comes another one of
*those* trucks with a boat

all over the
double yellow lines -

all up in the mustard.

I manage to squeeze by
and check my vibrating mirror
hoping to catch a glimpse
of the boat name
(just out of curiosity)

as it drifts away but
can't make it out.
In my mind it says
"Second Chance"
as we've both been

given another,
and suddenly,
I see them all,
every second chance,
the cars and trucks and boats alike,

all floating
in a sea of mustard.

*Someone Drugged My Tacos*


styrofoam ate my tacos
the sand swallowed me whole
popcorn on the ceiling
where did my body go

I was lying on a blanket
then digging in the sand
searching for my body
why was there popcorn on the ceiling

we had a picnic at the park
while counting popcorn on the ceiling
everything was fine
until I ate three steak tacos

I think someone drugged my tacos
the sand tried to eat me
as I searched for my kids toys
buried in the popcorn on the ceiling

I'm not sure what happened next
then I drifted to sleep
while counting all the raised bumps
falling from the popcorn-styled ceiling

*Chicken Nuggets*


These dinosaurs taste delicious, and
the crispy ghosts are even better.

*The Hungry Masseuse*

Have you ever heard
a masseuse's stomach growl
as you lie face down,
shoulders being rubbed,
their stomach by your ear?

The only thing more hilarious
is imagining them seeing yourself
through their eyes,
your body convulsing
while trying not to laugh.

*There Was Comfort in Our Couch...*

a place where family gathered
to watch late night movies
and eat popcorn,

a place that cured colds and the flu
and served as an extended stay
for long bouts of pneumonia,

a place you took with
when leaving the house behind
through a lengthy divorce,

a place you moved on from
in exchange for a single camping chair
with a built-in cup holder.

## Remain Calm

The doctors led us into
separate hospital rooms.

"Remain calm," they said,
and the cops walked in.

The cops questioned me
while jotting notes

in small notebooks,
and I imagine they

asked the same questions
to the rest of my family.

Something along the lines of,
"Does your dad beat you?"

I shook my head no,
never wanting to go back

to a hospital
again.

*Balconies*


I see your empty balconies.
Are you already off to work?

I gaze past the red cardinal
between branches neatly trimmed;
my parking lot view betrays you.

Maybe the strangers who reside
in these revolving boxes
take other forms of transportation,

I think to myself as storms roll in.
A thunderous drum beats awake
the brass melody of car alarms joined by flashing lights,

like trumpeting fireflies igniting a field at night.
I tap the baton, take a deep breath,
raise my hands high…

and it's over.
Too short,
this life.

Alarms and lights
fading one-by-one.
I know you're here.

My baton is the pen that now rests;

musical notes are the words captured on this page.
I bow down and hear no applause.

The cardinal sings a thank you song,
or so I'd like to believe.

Maybe someday you'll join me
on this balcony.

*Concrete Jungle*

I imagine mountains
where business buildings stand tall,

a clear blue ocean
poured over asphalt and concrete,

waves melodiously splashing
as the sound of nearby traffic

hits the sidewalk shore.
A plane roars overhead;

I look up and wonder,
*What brings the passengers here?*

*Raccoon Mountain*


The sun shines through gray rain clouds,
beams of light
ignite the dense cypress forest,

wet trees shimmer,
and the sandy, moss-topped forest floor
sparkles green and gold.

*The Dandelion Hunter*

A white flower head dandelion
bobs in pride area above green leaves fully fanged.
A zephyr pulls you from the pride.
Oh, nomadic seed traveling an unknown range.

There's no telling where the breeze may blow.
Yet in the night you hunt instinctively where others nary see.
Your dispersed seed will take root and grow;
from out the darkness you shall spring.

*Without a Poem on the Page*

The days have gone by
too quick to keep up with,
and before I know it

a month has passed
without
a poem on the page

as if nothing
has happened
at all.

polished typewriter
sounds like a black grand piano,
music to my ears

*Ember Soul*


A fire burns inside my soul.
It burns and churns and yearns to grow.
Nowhere for the flames to go,
it burns and burns and burns – then chokes.

Every ember losing its glow.
Nothing left for flames to show.
Every ember; every soul,
burns and burns and burns – then chokes.

snipers taking their
starting positions on the
surrounding rooftops

*Farmer's Almanac*

I wonder where they all disappear to
after abruptly taking over
the newsstands each year?

I find it unlikely that they all find
good homes with welcoming hands
to flip through their predictive pages.

Though, I must admit, every year
temptation brews within
as I consider picking one up.

Someday, I'll have a back pocket
dedicated just for you,
Farmer's Almanac.

*Attempting to Avoid Abduction*


It's a strange feeling
seeing all of my things
packed tightly
in the back of a U-Haul,

and even more strange
to see all of the
oncoming traffic
pulled over
to the side of the road
as I make my way across
the Midwest,

and even more strange still
to see drivers
exiting their vehicles,
phones pointed to the sky.

I check my mirrors
half-expecting an alien invasion
but instead (and maybe worse)
spot a tornado.

In the middle of farm country
with nowhere safe to turn for cover,
I decide to floor it,
my possessions and I
topping out at under 100 miles per hour,
attempting to avoid abduction.

*Can't Sleep*


Lying awake in bed,
while everyone else is long asleep,

wondering what we're going to do today and
whether I'll be awake for it.

No sign brought greater relief
than the one that read:

NO PHONE SERVICE
BEYOND THIS POINT

*LaSalle Metra Line*

I could hear the train horn blare
from my childhood home
the ding ding dinging bells
would soon follow.

Red and white
candy-cane striped gates
slowly drop down
as the train hisses to a stop.

Train cart doors slide open
as hurried passengers funnel in.

I dreamed of being among them,
having somewhere important to be,
finding my place in the big city.

Fast forward 30 years
and I just want a cabin in the woods.

I'll figure out the rest
once I get there.

*Cataloochee Valley*

Does anyone else
think it's ridiculous
that I'm sitting at a campfire
with a headlamp strapped
around my head
so that I can see
this poem
I'm writing
beneath the stars
in the Cataloochee Valley?

*I Am the Highway*


My three-year-old son picks up my phone
saying *I want to see,*
as I explain *It's music,*

*there is no video,*
*we listen with our ears.*
And I rest my eyes after a long day

and see everything,
while in the background
the music plays

*I am the sky*

*Unimpressionable*


I try my best to ensure you don't leave
an impression on me,
but it's instantaneous.

Upon realizing this,
I try my best to ensure you don't realize
you're leaving an impression

(do you realize?),
and now here you are
immortalized by pen and paper:

an everlasting impression.

*The Song Will Go On*


Silence…
like the cicadas
except more like

several weeks than
several years.
Quiet days,

quiet nights,
seemingly no poems
to write

until tonight
my mind
mysteriously awakens

prompting me to reach for
pen and paper,
and as the words begin to flow

in a rhythmic chorus
of rising highs and
falling lows

I can only hope
the song will go on
tomorrow.

*In a Garden of Poems*

Some poems seem to sprout
right through my
finger-gripped pen
and onto the page.

Others take more time
and careful tending to,
much like our family garden,
beginning as a simple idea,

the planting of a seed,
and with a lot of hard work
and a little bit of luck
words suddenly begin

to grow into vines.
After some decisive pruning
the squash is sectioned off
and climbing up the trellis,

leafy greens and herbs
are in their respective rows,
and the cucumbers are
ripe and ready

for the prying hands of children
who pluck them from the vine;
they eat them like popsicles
beneath the summer sun.

The kids seem to grow
much like the pumpkins,
a foot at a time
every second I look away.

I lay down my pen
to rest my cramped and calloused hand,
and lift my nose from the page,
wondering where I planted the carrots

and whether anyone will notice.
For a moment
I think, just maybe,
everything is right

before spotting a pumpkin
that snuck through the fence
and into my neighbor's yard
already a foot tall.

*Where is the Muse*


I find that it often appears in silence,
no tv, no mobile devices.
I quickly reach for pen and paper when it arrives

knowing it may not stay for long.
Maybe I should carve it into stone
instead of scribbling hurriedly onto this page,

but we both know that even stone tablets
can't contain it
for the muse travels at will

from vessel to vessel,
and as it leaves me, I wonder,
will it find its way to you?

Acknowledgments

A big thank you to my #1 fan, Carol Kean; thank you for your continued encouragement and support. A special thanks to my partner, Jessica, and our three kids: Damon, Declan, and Derek; thank you for your love and support (and for serving as occasional subjects for my poems). And thank you to my family and friends for your love and support - in the poetry world and/or life in general (and for also serving as occasional subjects for my poems).

Dear Reader,

Thank you for your time in reading my first full-length collection of poetry. This collection spans around 10-years' worth of writing: 2014'ish through 2024. I hope at least one of these poems resonated with you and stays with you throughout the years.

Choosing a title was a difficult task, and I decided on Anywhere Imaginable because that is the place I go to when writing poetry. One of my favorite things about reading poetry is that we're transported to that very same place; there's no telling where that next poem may take us.

I'd like to get another full-length collection out in the world someday but really don't know when. Until then, feel free to visit my site periodically at daviddemropoetry.com where you can also subscribe for updates.

As always, feel free to reach out if you'd like to connect, and remember, keep dreaming and keep chasing dreams!

Looking forward,
David Demro